GREAT HOUSES of CORNWALL

BY

Jean Stubbs

BOSSINEY BOOKS

First published in 1987 by
Bossiney Books
St Teath, Bodmin, Cornwall

Reprinted 1992

Printed by
Penwell Print Ltd,
Callington, Cornwall

ISBN 0 948158 33 6

Front Cover: Bicycling up from
Lanhydrock Gatehouse in the
late 1890s.
Back Cover: Looking down on
Trerice.
Title Page: Lanhydrock viewed
through the Gatehouse arch.

Acknowledgment

The Author and Publisher are deeply indebted to The National
Trust for making this book possible and for providing all the
photographs except for those specifically taken for this project
by Ray Bishop. They are also particularly appreciative of the
ready spirit of co-operation shown by Lord St Levan in allowing
valuable old photographs to be copied from the St Levan family
album.

Our debt also extends to Josephine Halloran whose diligent
and dedicated work as National Trust archivist has made her a
valuable contributor to the book.

Last but not least publisher Michael Williams and Bossiney
Books are profoundly grateful to Giles Clotworthy whose
initiative paved the way for this venture and who has been so
helpful in other enterprises involving The National Trust and
Bossiney.

Contents

OLD POST OFFICE
TINTAGEL

LANHYDROCK

COTEHELE

TRERICE

ANTONY

TRELISSICK

ST MICHAEL'S
MOUNT

About the Author and the Book

Born and educated in Lancashire, Jean Stubbs began writing seriously when both her children had started school and her marriage had failed. Her first novel *The Rose Grower,* published by Macmillan in 1962, was written mainly on the London underground on her way to work. She has since produced fifteen other novels and innumerable short stories, worked for two years for an industrial publisher, reviewed regularly for *Books & Bookmen,* frequently lectured and run discussion groups at seminars and writers' summer schools, and in 1984 was appointed Writer in Residence for Avon.

In 1973 she created 'the most memorable detective since Sherlock Holmes' with Inspector Lintott, who appeared in her trilogy of Victorian/Edwardian mysteries: *Dear Laura* (Book of the Month Club selection); *The Painted Face* and *The Golden Crucible.* These were followed by a quartet of novels, under the collective title *Brief Chronicles,* which followed the fortunes of a fictitious family — the Howarths of Lancashire — during the Industrial Revolution. The first volume,

Kit's Hill, was a Book Club selection in both England and the USA in 1979. This was followed by *The Ironmaster, The Vivian Inheritance* and *The Northern Correspondent.* Her latest and most recently published novel, *A Lasting Spring,* is a new departure, being neither mystery nor history and set in the period 1928 — 1945.

She was one of the first writers in the country to have a micro computer word-processor, which she finds invaluable for banking research and editing manuscripts. A Londoner for over twenty years, she moved to Cornwall with her second husband in 1975, and has lived there ever since in a two-hundred-year-old cottage.

In 1985, her first book for Bossiney, *100 Years Around the Lizard,* was published on Helston Flora Day. In this she not only toured one of the most magical areas in all Cornwall but, thanks to some wonderful old photographs, turned the calendars back.

Now in *Great Houses of Cornwall* Jean Stubbs explores seven National Trust properties. Digging deeply, perceptively into the history of

seven contrasting areas of Cornwall and the photographic archives of The National Trust, she reflects: 'They are different and yet they have so much in common. They all share a long history. Tendrils of kinship and friendship curl out and cling between house and house.'

As befits a highly talented novelist, she writes wisely too about the people who lived in these great houses: men who were Members of Parliament and High Sheriffs and wives who 'conducted households the size of small hotels'.

This book, thoughtful text and rich black and white photography — much of it old — all reek of nostalgia. 'This was an age in which everyone's position was clear and the rules were kept.'

Antony House, Cotehele, Lanhydrock House, The Old Post Office at Tintagel, 'a great house in its day', Trerice, Trelissick and St Michael's Mount, this is a brilliant Cornish tapestry — a grand tour in fact, and in Jean Stubbs we have a thoughtful guide and interpreter.

RIGHT Author Jean Stubbs at Lanhydrock.

GREAT HOUSES OF CORNWALL

Often in the summer the unexpected voice of an old friend on the telephone will hail us with excitement and delight, saying 'We're on holiday in Cornwall and thought we must be near you. Can we call in?' From where? Some town is mentioned, anything between fifty and a hundred miles away. A little pause follows. Then, 'Oh, we didn't realise it was so far . . .'

Cornwall is very far. A long far far away, as my grandson once said. And Cornwall is old and as full of history as Job was full of days. So I need not tell you that to wander through its great houses and gardens is to reach an understanding of patrician Cornwall through the centuries, and I shall not imply that this can be done quickly. These seven National Trust properties range from the border, through the middle of the county, up to the north coast, and down to the sea: from the Georgian elegance of Antony House to the mystical grandeur of St Michael's Mount. And each of them has a distinct character and a personal quality. To see one is not to see them all, and true appreciation is never hurried. I did once meet an American who had 'done' Cornwall in twenty four hours, but he was hoping to do Great Britain in a fortnight, and had no time to savour anything. I would advise a few days' tranquil tour and a thoughtful wending of the way home again; or a visit here and there when you can, taking care to miss none.

They are different and yet they have much in common. They all share a long history. Tendrils of kinship and friendship curl out and cling between house and house. Their people knew and visited and often married each other — Carew to Edgcumbe to Arundell — and the marriages meant more land and money. When Lady Catherine married the 3rd baronet Sir John St Aubyn she brought a dowry of £10,000 to the Mount, all in half-crowns and loaded onto two carts. Their owners were well-educated: Sir Richard Carew spoke six languages and in 1602 published his unique work *The Survey of Cornwall*. They were

ABOVE The Park at Lanhydrock.

RIGHT The carriage porch at Antony.

OVERLEAF Spring in West Cornwall. '. . . the mystical grandeur of St Michael's Mount.'

men of vision who improved and extended their properties; public-spirited citizens who played their parts as Members of Parliament and High Sheriffs; brave warriors who fought against their country's enemies and suffered divided loyalties in the Civil War. Their wives conducted households the size of small hotels, bore many children, entertained innumerable guests, looked handsome and never seemed hurried. These families had their portraits painted and their houses drawn by famous artists of the time, and later on compiled albums of photographs which are the domestic history of their time. Finally, in an age which proved unkind to owners of stately homes, they made sure that the house itself lived on — even though the family might not.

It seems appropriate to begin on our side of the Tamar, which is nearest to England and therefore most English in its aspects, and a happy choice because **Antony House** is still a family home occupied by the Carew Poles whose ancestor Sir William Carew built it in the early eighteenth century. In 1961 Sir John Carew Pole gave Antony House to the National Trust with an endowment. This Georgian mansion, dressed in silvery-grey Pentewan stone, stands gracefully in its formal gardens and conveys a pleasing sense of harmony and continuity. Inside, much of the furniture is original to the house.

The residents keep out of the way of our guided tour, while we peer into the shell of their private lives. We see traces of occupancy: photographs on the dressing-tables, books by the bed, Zip firelighters and matches by the library hearth. Public interest helps to keep Antony a family home, and yet the

BELOW Cotehele: '. . . a Medieval stronghold.'
We owe a considerable debt to The National Trust. In Cornwall alone it presides over acres of countryside, miles of coastline, as well as the houses and gardens.

ABOVE *The 5th Earl of Mount Edgcumbe on his horse outside the entrance to Cotehele in the 1930s.*

perceptive visitor must feel something of an intruder. Outside the sun is shining. This is an afternoon for tea on the lawn, a saunter round the garden walks, or a children's game of hide and seek among the topiary hedges. But today the visitors enjoy it while the owners stay indoors.

There is no family at **Cotehele,** though it displays a loving state of polish. In the armoured hall a golden mass of daffodils on the oak table. Geraniums flare in a bright brass bowl. A log fire leaps and crackles on the hearth, exuding a poignant scent of wood-smoke. The atmosphere is dramatically different. Cotehele is a Medieval stronghold, handsome and well-armed, feudal in contrast to the eighteenth-century elegance of Antony. A lovely up-and-down house, changing and adapting to the demands of different times, it possesses rooms and closets and alcoves to which its inmates could once retreat from the bustling centre. The walls of living and bedrooms are rich in tapestries, so rich that in the Bacchanalian Punch room one of them has been slit for the sake of convenience. But in the Jacobean Tower, where royalty has breakfasted and slept, the rooms are gracious and full of sunlight. The kitchen is surprisingly small and cosy for such a large establishment, more like that of an old farmhouse, with its high settle by the open hearth.

Outside, the garden has been created on many different levels and marks the different centuries as does the house. Once, Cotehele was a world unto itself, complete with flour mill, cider house, blacksmith's forge, carpenter and wheelwright's shops, a sawpit, the *Edgcumbe Arms* and its own quay. Now that world and its people are gone. The alarums and excursions are over, and this fortress is tranquil.

Most of the original **Lanhydrock House,** bought by Sir Richard Robartes of Truro and built by his son Sir John, was burned down in 1881, and what you see is a skilful early seventeenth-century pastiche. With the rebuilding of the house came the last flowering of the family, as the second Lord Robartes made manifest a Victorian dream of domestic bliss. Lanhydrock was not only to become a great house again but a great family, each of whose nine children had a recognisable family face: large-eyed, full-mouthed and fair-complexioned. And the house became a living entity in three tiers: master and mistress, the nursery, and a little army of indoor and outdoor servants.

This was an age in which everyone's position was clear and rules were kept. Floors and doors in the family's part of the house were made of oak, while those of their servants were made of pine. No member of the family ever entered the servants' quarters, ruled by the butler and housekeeper, and the strictest morality was observed in segregating male from female servants who had separate bedroom staircases.

The children's world was on the first floor of the south wing: self-contained even to the iron cage outside the passage window which held the nursery milk churn. And someone of imagination had ordained that the day nursery should overlook the stable yard and clock, so much more fascinating to young eyes than the finest landscapes.

A high-ceilinged kitchen, with gigantic basting spit, vast dressers and a long scrubbed wooden table was the centre of the servants' world. This culinary paradise, supplemented by a separate vegetable kitchen and scullery, supplied by its own fish, meat and dry larders, a bakehouse and dairy, catered for a host of stomachs. On the high marble table, like some dairy altar, a myriad of jellies and shapes could cool. How Mrs Beeton would have approved and envied the domestic equipment, from hot cupboard to bread-baking oven.

The most modern comforts and conveniences were installed. Central heating, an electric lighting plant, marble

BELOW The Hall at Trerice.

topped radiators, gilt brass light fittings, cast-iron baths with mahogany rims and plungers and claw feet, plate glass and William Morris wallpapers. The great house looked out onto a formal garden, and stood in a park of great beauty and dignity, and the continuity of the Agar-Robartes seemed assured.

Mary, Thomas, Everilda, Gerald, Victor, Violet, Constance, Cecil, Alexander. What a sheaf of arrows to aim at posterity! But of those five sons and four daughters, only two married and only one had a child. The First World War ended the life of Thomas, the heir. Social changes brought about by the Second World War ended the life of Lanhydrock as a home. That late-Victorian renaissance had been the final flowering of a great family.

In the wild kingdom of Cornwall's north coast it is easy to believe that **Tintagel** was the legendary birthplace of King Arthur, unsurprising that three popular Victorian poets lauded its magical beauty, and fairly obvious that crowds of people would then want to see it for themselves. In its effort to accommodate visitors, the village demolished its old buildings and put up new ones, and we are fortunate that the **The Old Post Office** escaped destruction. This Medieval dwelling was probably built as a small manor house in the fourteenth century

UPPER Looking across the River Fal to Trelissick. '. . . the surrounding park and woods are there for our delight.'

LOWER Trelissick House — '. . . a house within a house'.

and is a highly individual example of vernacular architecture. At first glance, with its squat shape and undulating roof, it looks like an illustration by Arthur Rackham to a fairy tale by the Brothers Grimm. The interior promises to be dark and poky. Instead it is light, unexpectedly spacious, and modestly dignified — a wonderful surprise inside and out.

Trerice has many layers of living, and keeps its secrets to itself. Originally a Medieval building, whose barn was combined with the house, the roofline has altered, and though experts can make educated guesses, no one really knows how it looked in the beginning. Rebuilt on a traditional English plan in the shape of an 'E' — a frequent architectural compliment to Good Queen Bess during her reign — this mellow and secluded manor retains the spirit of graceful welcome it must once have extended to visiting country squires. Wonderfully lit by its huge east window, the hall rises through two storeys of the house. Most of

LEFT *Family and friends at Lanhydrock at the turn of the century.*

14

the window panes are original, and though mending has resulted in different colours and thicknesses of glass these in no way spoil the general effect. Sadly, a number of panes have been cracked by aircraft on their flight paths down the west coast of England, inflicting more damage in a few years than age could inflict in hundreds.

This was an Arundell house for four centuries, but in post-Arundell days it passed from hand to hand, and from private to public ownership, and the estate was divided into small farms. When the National Trust bought it in the Coronation Year of Queen Elizabeth the Second — which seems appropriate — it had the appearance of a run-down farm, with its wilderness of a garden and shabby buildings. In the restoration of the house, the spirit of Trerice lives again, and Trerice is a great spirit.

A house within a house, **Trelissick** was designed by Edmund Davy, grandfather of Sir Humphry Davy, and built about 1750 by a good-natured, sociable and eccentric gentleman called John Lawrence. Half a century later the estate was bought by one of the richest men in Cornwall, Guinea-a-minute Daniell, and in 1825 his son Thomas built a grander house round the earlier one. Trelissick itself is a private home and not open to the public, but the surrounding park and woods are there for our delight.

St Michael's Mount is a palimpsest: a manuscript on which the original writing has been effaced to make room for the next story. And yet it is not effaced, for you can walk from one story to another in the castle today, and all of them live contentedly together.

'*Lofty, rocky, inaccessible . . .*' was the description of St Michael's Mount by John Taylor the Water Poet, and he added that it was not worth the taking nor the keeping, but in that he was wrong. The Mount in its time has played so many valuable parts: an ancient trading station and thriving harbour; a Medieval church and priory; a garrison and Royalist stronghold; and finally a private house. For the last, as well as the first of our great houses, is a home, which has belonged to the St Aubyn family since 1659.

Spiritual legend touched it in the year 495 when a group of fishermen had a vision of the archangel St Michael standing on a perilous ledge of rock, high above the sea. Magical legend has lived on in the Giant Cormoran who was trapped in a pit by a Cornish lad called Jack, who became known locally as *Jack-the-Giant-Killer*. Historical legend is manifest in the beacon on its church tower which flared forth in 1587 to herald the coming of the Armada, and the sight of 130 Spanish galleons must have been an awesome one. In humbler capacity its Moorstone

BELOW The Old Post Office at Tintagel.

Lantern has shone out to guide the fishing boats back to harbour. And on great occasions such as the Queen's Silver Jubilee the castle is floodlit.

Durability and adaptability are virtues of the Mount. Its church has been devastated by an earthquake, decimated by the Black Death, sacked during the Reformation, and is still a hallowed place for public worship, and for prayer and pilgrimage. Its walls, once besieged by war, are still besieged by water and wild weather, but they continue to protect the house and home within.

Rich in history and legend, the castle by day rises from the sea like a picture in a children's fairy tale, and by night like some fairy ship, lit and ready for the voyage.

ABOVE Josephine Halloran, while archivist at the National Trust in Cornwall, established the photographic archive. A graduate in History of Art and Drama, she is currently administrator/archivist on the National Trust's Vernacular Buildings Survey in Cornwall.

ANTONY

BELOW An aerial view of Antony taken in the 1960s. Since then, the greenhouses have been removed and the tennis court resited.

ABOVE RIGHT The South Front and Park of Antony, looking down from Bowling Green Hill.

RIGHT The Cupola and
Arcade on the South Front.
These brick wings, which
enclose the forecourt, were
added to the house soon
after its completion.

ABOVE Around 1933, when this ornate garden still flowered and one could see through the wrought-iron screen to the River Lynher, the young Elizabeth Carew Pole and three canine friends had their photograph taken one fine morning.

BELOW The freestanding Claire Voie may be seen from the South side of the house like a frieze of stiff black lace, gracing a vista near Bowling Green Hill. Copied from eighteenth-century gates at Beddington Manor in Surrey, home of Sir Nicholas Carew, it was resited in 1947.

LEFT A further improvement, in 1850, was the granite Porte-Cochere which provided a covered carriage porch and an outer hall. The hall was intended to keep out draughts, but is also a large, light and lovely place in which to sit.

ABOVE The North Front of Antony House. Between 1890 - 1905, Sir Reginald Pole-Carew made radical alterations to the East Wing and created this formal garden. Neither of these changes was to last. In 1947 the East Wing was demolished, so returning the house to its original eighteenth-century appcarance. And the garden, whose upkeep had become prohibitive, was transformed into a long lawn which swept up to the foot of the terrace.

BELOW Photographed from the air in the 1930s, in its pride and prime, the stylised beauty of Sir Reginald's garden is formed by clipped box hedges, shaped flower beds, deep borders and topiary dwarf evergreens. The walling is elaborate, the gate-piers graceful, and at that time three vistas, framed by trees, led down to the River Lynher.

LEFT Now terraces and a daisied lawn lead down to the river.

RIGHT The exquisite detail of a Rainwater Head on the facade of the house.

LEFT With a portrait of King Charles I over the chimney-piece, and another of King Charles II to his right, this seems to be the Hall of a Royalist family, but Sir Richard Carew's sympathies were with Parliament, and his two sons followed suit. John Carew, one of the judges at the King's trial was later executed for regicide, and Alexander was beheaded because he changed sides at the wrong time.

BELOW LEFT The Hall is panelled in Dutch oak, and leads to an Inner Hall and grand staircase.

BELOW This charming water-colour was painted by an unknown artist in the early nineteenth century, and shows the magnificent staircase which is lit by the original glass candle globes.

LEFT The Dining Room, wood-panelled, with a harmonious mixture of eighteenth and nineteenth-century furniture, has an air of comfort as well as elegance.

RIGHT There is much to admire in the Saloon, from the Waterford glass chandelier to the paintings by Joshua Reynolds, but don't miss the view from the three windows down to the estuary of the Lynher.

LEFT   On the walls of the staircase, and along the first floor corridor hang portraits of the Carew and Pole families from different centuries, and at the west end is a study of the present Carew Pole family painted in 1985. On either side of the corridor bedroom doors stand open, providing glimpses of painted panelling and four-poster beds.

RIGHT The painted panelling in some rooms has been stripped to show the beauty of the wood. You see an example of this in the Porch Room. Daphne du Maurier, the Westcountry novelist, slept here once, and was inspired by the portrait of Rachel Carew — next to the door — to write *My Cousin Rachel*. But inspiration does not mean faithful reproduction, and Rachel in the novel was not Rachel in the portrait.

LEFT The portrait of Sir Alexander Carew, by an unknown artist, hangs on the wall between the Inner and Outer Library. Following the political convictions of his father, he outraged the Royalist wing of his family by holding Drake's Island in Plymouth Sound for Parliament in the Civil War. Then, long and heavily besieged by the King's army, and wondering if perhaps he had backed the wrong side, he changed his mind and was executed for treachery. Even on the scaffold he seemed to be uncertain about anything but his death, which was apparently the best solution to a sorry puzzle. But his Royalist relatives, who had previously slashed his portrait from its frame and despatched it to the cellar, now decided that he had been martyred for the King, brought it out and stitched it roughly back again — as you can see!

RIGHT Lady Anne Carew was the only daughter of 4th Earl of Coventry and brought a handsome dowry with her when she married Sir William Carew in 1713. Her portrait, painted by Michael Dahl, hangs on the staircase wall.

RIGHT Sir John Carew Pole, dressed in a page's uniform for the Coronation of King George V in 1911, was nine years old when Francis Bacon painted this portrait, which hangs in the Green Bedroom.

COTEHELE

Cotehele, with its extensive grounds and estates, belonged to the Edgcumbe family for nearly six hundred years.

BELOW A Spring welcome to Cotehele. A host of golden daffodils leads to the Gatehouse . . .

LEFT   . . . and coming out into the sunshine, during a Royal Visit to Cotehele on 16 July, 1985, is Prince Philip, the Duke of Edinburgh. The Gatehouse which leads to the Hall Court, is part of additions built in the sixteenth century by Sir Piers Edgcumbe, who was rich and married riches, and so completed the building operations begun by his father Sir Richard, warrior and man of vision, who is a legendary figure in Cornish history.

RIGHT The East Front
before major alterations took
place in 1862, showing the
Medieval structure.

LEFT Once this fifteenth-
century barn was simply part
of the old farmyard. Fully
restored, it now serves quite
a different purpose.

RIGHT The dome-shaped roof of this Medieval Dovecote in the Valley Garden collapsed in 1860 and was restored by the National Trust. Here it is being rebuilt in 1962. Now it houses a family of white doves. You can just see the Medieval stewpond by its side. In winter the pond and dovecote were major sources of fresh food for the household.

BELOW A welcome tea-break in the late nineteenth century. Workers at the old lime kilns on Cotehele Quay standing still for a while. The sign on the house at the left is the Edgcumbe Arms, once a public house for the local population, now a tea-house for the visitors.

BELOW RIGHT Looking down on Cotehele Quay and over the Tamar, showing the lime kilns and the old boathouse in the late nineteenth century.

RIGHT The 6th Earl of Mount Edgcumbe and his wife, who came to live at Cotehele around 1940, with some of their many tenants.

BELOW RIGHT An earlier photograph of the 6th Earl, sitting centre front, with sappers in charge of all search lights at Plymouth during the First World War.

BELOW Lady Edith, wife of the 5th Earl of Mount Edgcumbe, taking a carriage drive through Cotehele estate in the 1920s.

LEFT Looking through the South Front entrance to the Great Hall door.

FAR RIGHT Sir Piers Edgcumbe's finest achievement is the early sixteenth-century Great Hall at Cotehele, seen here in pristine condition in 1954. Refectory table, armour and weapons are seventeenth century. Pewter plates and mugs are eighteenth century and bear the Mount Edgcumbe arms.

RIGHT The Great Hall at Cotehele laid up for tenants' supper on Lady Day at the end of the last century.

LEFT When the east wing was reconstructed in 1862 a bay window was added to the New Drawing Room, which had been part of the old servants quarters, and is almost an exact reproduction of a room which had been there before. The roof is copied from the original which had fallen into decay.

LEFT Combining comfort with elegance the Punch Room was a convivial and masculine place. Motifs of drinking are everywhere. Soho tapestries depict Bacchanalian scenes, and one of them has been slit to allow for a door opening into the Old Dining Room. And if you inspect the door of the little wine cellar you will see that air-holes form the shape of a bunch of grapes.

RIGHT The beauty of sunlight and linenfold panelling in the Old Drawing Room. The interior porch was created in 1627 when the Jacobean tower was constructed.

BELOW Forming the second storey of the Jacobean tower, the Old Drawing Room is dignified and impressive.

LEFT An eighteenth-century
portrait of Lady Edgcumbe,
wife of Admiral George,
Lord Edgcumbe and
daughter of Gilbert
Archbishop of York,
engraved by Samuel
Reynolds.

ABOVE The White Room is hung with Mortlake tapestries and forms the basement apartment of the tower. The seventeenth-century four-poster bed is hung with embroidered linen.

LEFT On the floor above the Punch Room, the Red Room forms part of the fourteenth-century additions to Cotehele, though furnished in late seventeenth-century style. The set of three tapestry panels was woven in Antwerp.

LEFT This is how the kitchen would have looked in Tudor times with its range of utensils. The meat rack has been hung with imitation carcases to give a realistic effect, and a garden basket filled with mock vegetables. The wide kitchen hearth is complete with pot hooks, iron kettle and pan and a chimney crane.

ABOVE And here are the Servants at Cotehele, photographed in the Hall Court, sometime during the late nineteenth century. Mr Paddon the butler is seated centre front, with the housekeeper on his right.

LEFT And this was where the family and servants
worshipped. The fifteenth-century Chapel is as old as its
clock and many of the original fittings have survived.

ABOVE When I was there an horologist had come to inspect
the Chapel Clock which was installed by Sir Richard
Edgcumbe five hundred years ago, and I saw it in all its
Tudor glory. The original mechanism still works, and the
clock, which has no face, still chimes. I know, because I
heard it.

LANHYDROCK

FAR RIGHT An aerial view of Lanhydrock and its estate. Originally a possession of the Medieval priory of St Petroc at Bodmin, Lanhydrock was bought by Sir Richard Robartes, merchant and banker of Truro, in 1620, and he began to build a new house on the site.

ABOVE Lanhydrock House seen from the Gatehouse. Sir Richard died in 1634 but his son John took up the task, finishing the new house eight years later. It was a quadrangular building, symmetrical as befitted the classical fashion of the day, but essentially Elizabethan in its detail. Around 1780, the East Wing was demolished, giving much more light to the rest of the house.

ABOVE Lanhydrock and the Garden. In 1857 the fashionable architect of the day, George Gilbert Scott, enlarged and remodelled the house and landscaped the garden. Woods were planted round the house, connected with carriage drives. This was in the time of the first Lord and Lady Robartes, who presided over Lanhydrock for more than forty years.

LEFT   Detail of a seventeenth-century Ballin bronze urn in the parterre. These urns once formed part of Lord Hertford's collection at Chateau de Bagatelle in the Bois de Boulogne.

ABOVE The Great Fire. On 4 April, 1881, most of
Lanhydrock House was consumed by a fire which began in
the old kitchen. The first Lady Robartes, then sixty-eight, was
successfully rescued by ladder from an upstairs window. She
survived the fire but not the shock, dying a few days later,
and the following year her husband died also. The second
Lord Robartes — 'the little lord' as he was called — restored
the church dedicated to St Petroc, as a memorial to his
parents. The font is also a memorial, to his fifth child John
Agar-Robartes, born in 1884, who died at the age of six
months.

LEFT The second Lord and Lady Robartes, who married in 1878, are seen here with their four eldest children: Mary (far left) born in 1879; the twins Thomas and Everilda (far right) born in 1880; and Gerald (on his mother's lap) born in 1883. Thomas, heir to Lanhydrock, was a bachelor of thirty-four when the First World War broke out. In 1915 he died of wounds received while rescuing a comrade at the Battle of Loos. Mary did not marry until 1919, when she was nearly forty. Her husband was Canon Yarde Buller.

ABOVE The four youngest Agar-Robartes, seated in a carriage outside the main entrance. From left to right: Violet, 1888 - 1965, never married, and lived at Lanhydrock all her life. Constance, 1890 - 1936, never married. She suffered from a mild disability in the form of a crooked back, but became a nurse and ran a nursing home in Wimbledon. Cecil, 1892 - 1939, never married. A Captain in the Rifle Brigade and then in the Tank Corps during the First World War, he suffered from diabetes, and died in a coma. On the carriage step holding a dog, is Alexander, 1895 - 1930, also never married. A Captain in the Lifeguards during the First World War, he was invalided out with shell-shock and an appalling facial disfigurement. For some years after the war he lived in London, attended by a male nurse, but committed suicide in 1930 by throwing himself from a high window.

ABOVE Lanhydrock was always a Liberal stronghold. This group photograph was taken on the Church steps when Mr Gladstone visited Lanhydrock in 1889.

ABOVE RIGHT Mary, 2nd Lady Robartes, in Coronation Robes. Lady Mary's duties and commitments were diverse and demanding. A devoted wife, mother of a large family, director of a large household and a hospitable hostess, she also had an important role to play in society.

FAR RIGHT ABOVE Portrait of a lady in a dashing hat. In 1899 Lord Robartes succeeded to the Viscountcy of Clifden. In this portrait, taken around 1905, his wife is entitled Lady Clifden.

RIGHT Lady Robartes Room. From this feminine sitting room, which must have been both office and private sanctuary, Lady Robartes directed the lives and routine of a household the size of a small hotel.

The gentlemen of the house had their own sanctuaries. The Smoking Room is a comfortable place in which the male Agar-Robartes and their male guests could relax and smoke and talk. And should the conversation languish they could always have a game of billiards.

LEFT While the BBC films his programme in March 1981, the late Arthur Negus, recounting the history of Pool, Billiards and Antiques, enjoys a game with professional player Ray Reardon.

BELOW LEFT The windows of the Billiard Room overlook one of the finest views of the grounds. The Victorian Billiard Table was built by Burroughs and Watts.

BELOW Though this photograph is referred to as *His Lordship's Bathroom,* there is reason to believe that Lord Robartes installed it for the use of his wife rather than himself. Apparently he preferred the old-fashioned comfort of a saucer-bath in front of the fire, which you can see in the adjoining bedroom.

OVERLEAF Lanhydrock today from the Park.

BELOW Lord Clifden holding a bicycle, with an affectionate Eva (the family's name for Everilda) and musical young Cecil in the gardens at Lanhydrock at the turn of the century.

ABOVE From left to right: Violet, Constance, Cecil and Alexander — the four youngest Agar-Robartes children — in the garden about 1905.

BELOW A family group, taken around 1902. Lord and Lady Clifden with their nine children. The Agar-Robartes were close, so close that no one appeared to leave home. The daughters look charming and eminently marriageable, but we continue to see them in family groups or about their own pursuits in Lanhydrock.

RIGHT Alexander with Constance, Everilda and Violet.

RIGHT Alexander in cricket gear.

LEFT Alexander batting and Victor wicket-keeping. A game of cricket in Lanhydrock forecourt about 1902.

BELOW From left to right: Victor, two charming young friends, Everilda and Gerald at Lanhydrock cricket ground around 1900.

Long hours and small wages were the lot of servants at this time, even in a benevolent household such as Lanhydrock, but the best and latest equipment had been installed in their working quarters when the house was rebuilt.

ABOVE RIGHT One of the servants at Lanhydrock photographed outside the kitchen quarters, holding two kittens, 1900.

ABOVE The kitchen at Lanhydrock, rebuilt in 1883, two years after the Great Fire, was regarded as a fine example of modern equipment and hygiene, a fitting place in which to produce the *haute cuisine* of a great house.

BELOW Nowdays the beauty of the Gallery and its ceiling is revealed, but the Victorians and Edwardians did love a cultured clutter. Here is the gallery as it was around 1910.

War has been declared. A way of life is over. The Agar-Robartes, like millions of other people, will pay a heavy price for defending their country.

ABOVE Victor Agar-Robartes, outside an army Orderly Room. A Major in the Grenadier Guards.

BELOW Cecil, seated (near left) in the Officers' Mess. A Captain in the Rifle Brigade and then in the Tank Corps.

The War is over. It has cost Lord Clifden the life of his eldest son and heir, and the health and happiness of his youngest son. Mary has married, but his other daughters — now approaching early middle-age — are still living at home. Lady Robartes died in 1921 and her second daughter Eva (Everilda) has taken her mother's place at Lanhydrock. Over this gradually dwindling household she will preside for nearly half a century, dying the last of all the children, in 1969.

ABOVE Lord Clifden in the late 1920s, with Violet on his right, Gerald the heir-apparent on his left, and Victor standing behind them.

ABOVE Now in his forties, spruce and military-looking,
Victor Agar-Robartes stands proudly in front of the first car.
Victor, the sixth child, broke the family mould. He lived
away from Lanhydrock, married twice and had a daughter.
This photograph was taken in the 1930s.

The second World War and the advent of evacuees must
have been a shock, but the Agar-Robartes no doubt extended
the hospitality of the house with their usual grace. Of the
original brood of children only three remained at
Lanhydrock. Gerald the 7th Viscount, Everilda, and Violet.
They could not cope with the problems caused by the black-
out, and the Hall became 'the room we sit in'.

BELOW Lanhydrock evacuees, playing bowls, 1940.

ABOVE A dynasty has ended. A domestic vision has
vanished. But Lanhydrock stands as a reminder of the Agar-
Robartes family in its late-Victorian days of glory. And the
magnolia still blooms.

ABOVE The Park at Lanhydrock in the spring of 1987.
Planting of trees began over two hundred years ago. Then in
the nineteenth century the first Baron Robartes planted
woods, connected by carriage drives, for miles around the
house. The great gale of December, 1979 blew down some
three hundred trees at Lanhydrock, but many of these have
been replanted.

LEFT Visitors walk along the avenue to Lanhydrock today.

THE OLD POST OFFICE
—TINTAGEL—

BELOW The Old Post Office at the turn of the century. No-one knows the original name of this dwelling, which was built as a small fourteenth-century manor house, but its present name harks back to 1844, when one room was rented to the General Post Office to receive letters, and served the village of Tintagel for almost fifty years.

RIGHT In 1901, with funds raised by public appeal, the National Trust bought the Old Post Office for £100. As one of the few surviving Cornish Medieval hallhouses, its individual character and undulating roof have been carefully preserved. The front of the building resembles an illustration to Grimm's Fairy Tales, but don't miss the back of the house, which is equally evocative. The neat grass lawn on the photograph has now been converted to a most delightful little garden, and near the compost heap is a model of the Old Post Office created by Mr R. G. Climo in 1950 and given to the National Trust eight years later.

OVERLEAF The Old Post Office and Tintagel High Street as it was in 1894 before the cottages were pulled down and the village street became a thoroughfare.

ABOVE This photograph of a Liberal gathering for Gladstone's visit to Cornwall was taken around 1890 by a Dr Allridge, who was an authority on Tintagel. The little village had been lifted from obscurity by its connection with the legendary King Arthur, who was supposed to have been born here. Three Victorian romantic poets extolled the legend in verse, and Tintagel became so popular that it tore down its old-fashioned cottages in order to build accommodation for interested visitors. The Old Post Office itself went up for auction in 1895 and was only saved by a group of artists, who bought it and made sure that it was repaired and preserved.

ABOVE The Hall rises from stone flagged floor to smoke-blackened roof. When the National Trust took over the house, it was empty. Its present simple furniture, nicely in keeping with the house, comes from old farms and cottages. To the right of the iron kettle on the hob is an old baking oven.

BELOW This bedchamber, which looks out onto the High Street through its two-light window, has more furniture in it now than when the photograph was taken. Three samplers, one of them an exotic ship in full sail, adorn the walls. On the oak bedstead which came from a farm house on Bodmin Moor, one corner of the feather mattress is turned back to show a bed-stock strung with hemp rope, as most beds were before the introduction of spring bases.

LEFT The Parlour Chamber, sparely furnished but cheerful and even comfortable enough, seems less important and certainly less private than the other bedroom. It opens out of a stairway, and to the left of the picture are the steep slate slabs by means of which you reach the narrow Gallery overlooking the Hall. They are not suitable for short, old or stiff legs!

ABOVE And here is the Old Post Room, now furnished in the style of a Victorian village post office and acting as a National Trust Shop.

RIGHT When a parcel post was introduced in the 1880s the postman had need of more than a sack. So Victorian ingenuity invented this 'Centre Cycle' and Victorian wit nicknamed it 'The Hen and Chickens'.

LEFT Tintagel had Letter Post in the 1840s, Parcel Post in the 1880s, and Telegraph Wires in the 1890s. This telephone beside the Post Room counter is known as a Spagnolettis receiver and undulator, and is the same type as that used by Tintagel's Sub-Postmaster, William Cobbledick Balkwill, in the late nineteenth century.

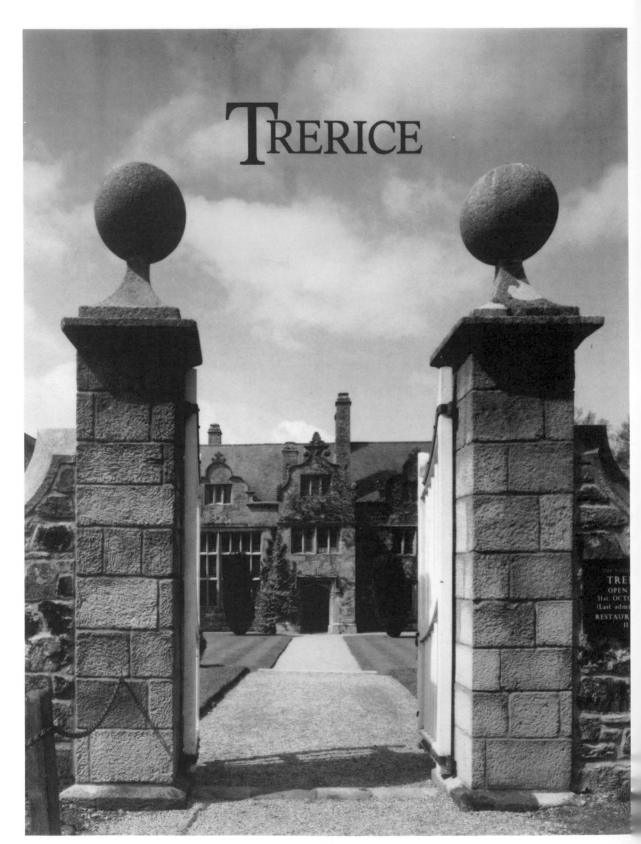

TRERICE

LEFT The first glimpse of Trerice through the front gate. The granite caps and balls of the gate piers were brought here when the Launceston bypass demolished their original home at Tresmarrow in 1975. They are as fortunate as this unique Elizabethan manor house, which remains almost unchanged because a series of owners maintained it while living elsewhere. Had it fallen into the hands of eighteenth or nineteenth-century Cornish gentry, who were making a fortune out of tin and copper, it could well have been pulled down or altered out of recognition.

ABOVE Age and weather have transformed the local limestone facade from yellow to silvery-grey. The scrollwork is Dutch in appearance and unique in Cornwall. Two very old granite lions, so well-worn as to resemble much-loved teddy bears, have kept guard over three great houses. They, too, are refugees from twentieth-century progress and much travelled. Originally they lived at Kenegie, a house of the Arundell family at Gulval, near Penzance. Then early in the nineteenth century they were moved to Lifton in Devon. In 1973, threatened by a scheme to widen the road, they were brought here by the National Trust.

RIGHT Looking down on to
the front entrance.

BELOW Around 1905 Kestle Mill Wesleyan Sunday School,
all dressed in its Sunday Best, had an Outing on Trerice
Moor, and of course visited Trerice itself, in whose gardens
they were duly photographed.

ABOVE This photograph of the south elevation of Trerice, showing the old Dutch garden, was taken about 1910. Since then the blocked windows have been restored to light, and the Dutch Garden has been replaced by grass and fruit trees which are set out in the *quincunx* pattern — every tree is in line with its neighbours, from whichever direction it is viewed. Just by the garden wall a little walk, lined with pink mallows, leads to a garden seat. It is a pleasing and tranquil place in which to stroll or sit, and there is a tempting display of plants for sale outside the shop.

LEFT The North Wing had gradually decayed and in 1860, after a severe gale, was judged to be unsafe, and taken down to the level of the string course — a granite line along the wall of the building. The Dutch scrollwork however, was saved for future use. Almost a century later, in 1954, Mr J. F. Elton who was then the National Trust's tenant, restored the North Wing completely and faithfully. In this photograph, taken in 1956, stonemasons are preparing blocks for the building works.

LEFT The work of restoration is almost done . . .

... and this is how the Back Court looked when they had finished.

LEFT Between 1982 and 1983 the lay-out of the court was altered. The circular grass bed was removed and a stone wall built.

LEFT Welcome to Trerice! As usual in manor houses of this plan you enter by a Screens Porch and Passage . . .

BELOW . . . and come into the Hall, the great room of the house. Yet this hall, rising through two storeys of the house, has an air of sociability rather than formal grandeur, and a wonderful mellow light streams in from the great east window. The plaster ceiling is decorative, bearing the initials of Sir John Arundell who transformed a Medieval house into an Elizabethan manor, and those of his wife Katharine and his sister Margaret. The table is the only piece of furniture which actually belonged to the house, although it was not made for the Hall until the late nineteenth century.

ABOVE The great mullioned and transomed east window contains 576 panes of glass. Much of the glass is original, but different colours and thicknesses show careful mending. This photograph shows Jim Swingler's restoration work on the leaded lights of the Hall window in 1986.

BELOW Trerice Library has the air of a masculine preserve, dignified and easy as becomes a room for work and thought. In fact it has had different functions and faces, and endured much alteration. Part of the former Medieval dwelling, it was re-fashioned by Sir John Arundell and given a semi-circular bay in the sixteenth century. In the early nineteenth century it was divided into two rather awkward little sitting-rooms. Only in 1969 was the library restored to its original size and elegant proportions by the National Trust.

LEFT Trerice Drawing Room, once the Medieval High Chamber, is a beautiful place facing due south and drenched with light from the semi-circular bay window. It possesses some of the loveliest features in the house, especially the ornate barrel ceiling and frieze which dominate the room. Most of the furniture is now eighteenth century. Also, I liked the dummy-board figures, one on each side of the fireplace, and the homely touch in the date on the overmantel ANNO.DOMINI:MCCCCCXX3 — where the plasterer realised too late that he should have left room for a Roman III.

The North Wing is reached by means of an extremely pretty connecting corridor, whose ceiling plasterwork has been restored, and from which two modern staircases were removed in the 1950s. In the small musicians' gallery you can peep into the hall through a row of arched apertures. The acoustics are said to be wonderful, and presentday musicians have played there delightfully.

BELOW The windows of the North Chamber look out onto the Back Court, but the first thing you notice on entering the room is this majestic tester bed of the 1760s.

ABOVE The Great Barn is great indeed, and as stately in its own way as any room in Trerice. A yellow flag, embroidered with a brilliant Cornish Chough, hangs here in memory of a renowned battalion of the Home Guard nicknamed *The Choughs*. In the long hot summer of 1940 when Britain faced invasion, local volunteers gathered at Trerice as they had gathered in the Napoleonic War, prepared to defend their country. The lawn within the back entrance gate, on which they drilled, was then known as the 'Parade Ground'.

RIGHT Nowadays the barn is a restaurant: a fitting place in which to end the tour of a great house, to rest and refresh yourselves, and absorb what you have seen.

TRELISSICK

LEFT At the head of Falmouth Harbour, set like a jewel in 376 acres of woods and parkland, Trelissick has marvellous views, looking down the deep water anchorage of Carrick Roads to the sea. The headland is now overgrown, but in this post-war photograph, looking west from Turnaware Point, you can see the jetties the U.S. Army used in 1944 for Operation Overlord.

ABOVE An engraving of the South Front of Trelissick by T. Allom, in 1831. The original house was rebuilt by a prolific architect called Peter Frederick Robinson, based on the plan of *Villa No. 3* in a book entitled *Designs for Ornamental Villas,* which he published in 1827. Note the cresting on the single-storeyed wings.

ABOVE When Trelissick changed hands in the mid-nineteenth century a second storey was added to the wings, and the simple elegance of Robinson's design was lost. This photograph taken about 1900 shows Victorian workmen in their long aprons, possibly making alterations to the ground floor sash windows and the interior of the house.

RIGHT The ship of Sir Humphrey Gilbert, discoverer of Newfoundland, was named *Squirrel,* and a squirrel is the family's crest. From 1844 to 1913 Trelissick was in the possession of the Gilbert family, and about 1860 a squirrel weathervane stood on top of the Water Tower. Here is Mr J. Dawson of the Bristol firm I. Dawson & Sons (Restorations Ltd) holding the Gilbert Squirrel prior to its being re-gilded in 1981.

Gardens, like houses, have their great moments. The Daniells, father and son, laid out the major features, with parkland which reaches down to the water's edge and carriage-roads which drive for miles through lovely hanging woods of beech, oak and pine. Their work was continued by the Gilbert family who did more planting and introduced some highly exotic species. But it was Mr and Mrs Ronald Copeland, inheriting Trelissick in 1937, who created a garden of outstanding beauty. By the mid-1970s it was at its peak, then extreme weather conditions — drought, frosts and storms — killed or damaged a vast number of shrubs and trees. Replanting began immediately and in the spring of 1987 *The Cornwall Garden Society Festival* was held here, to celebrate the 75th birthday of the society, and the garden looked beautiful.

FAR RIGHT A delightful Victorian photograph showing a man standing beneath the leaves of a giant gunnera in Trelissick Garden. Taken about 1900.

RIGHT The lily pond. Another picture taken around 1900.

LEFT Trelissick Water Tower, built about 1860. In the last century the hazards of a great fire — such as that suffered by Lanhydrock in 1881 — were met by a Merryweather fire engine, a fire-brigade formed from staff on the estate, and a Water Tower connected to an underground tank system. Nowadays, mains water is supplied, and the Water Tower has been transformed into a holiday cottage by the National Trust.

ABOVE One of Trelissick's panoramic views looking southwards to the River Fal, with Channals Creek on the left.

St Michael's Mount

ABOVE 'Lofty, rocky, inaccessible . . . ' wrote John Taylor, the
Water poet. St Michael's Mount in different moods. This
stormy scene was engraved in 1813 by W. B. Cooke, from a
drawing by J. M. Turner.

RIGHT And this coloured steel engraving, 1863, from T.
Nelson's *Views in Cornwall* shows people crossing the
causeway. The Mount has been a place of pilgrimage since
the year 495 when a group of fisherman had a vision of the
archangel St Michael standing on a perilous ledge now
known as *St Michael's Chair*.

The Mount is a world within itself and a family home, as depicted by these photographs of past and present.

ABOVE The present Lord and Lady St Levan.

RIGHT The Hon. Giles St Aubyn L.V.O. and the parents of the present Lord St Levan, with their dogs Karola and Ben.

FAR RIGHT Ranks of St Aubyns. An unusual and powerful composition which gives an impression of the strength and solidarity of family life at the turn of the century.

ABOVE A world in itself, the Mount takes care of itself. A fire in an island castle must obviously be dealt with on the spot, and by everybody available. Ready for such an emergency, the ladies of the Mount and villagers stand by Lillie the Fire engine while the firemen stand back.

RIGHT Villagers. This charming study of women and children in the courtyard below the Mount was taken by Herbert Hughes in 1895. In the busy days of the harbour there were 53 houses on the island and about 300 villagers.

RIGHT When the causeway is covered the crossing must be made by boat. Here are the Mount Boatmen in the family livery, which was designed in the eighteenth century. You can see one of these costumes in the Museum Room.

BELOW RIGHT Crossing the water for another purpose. Castles must be cleaned, and this delightful little sketch shows the family being rowed ashore. The housekeeper in charge of the operations at that time was called Mrs Miners.

BELOW But now the world outside comes to see the world inside. These relaxed and cheerful sea cadets were photographed outside the newly built Sail Loft Restaurant and National Trust Shop in 1985. When the harbour was a thriving place these buildings used to be the blacksmith's and carpenter's shops, and the yard was used for boat repairs.

RIGHT Visitors tend to accept the high state of polish in great houses, and polishers remain invisible, but here we see 'Mrs Shine' making a mirror of the table. The Chevy Chase Room is so named because of its plaster frieze of legendary animals, but this used to be the monastery refectory and in spite of its dashing name and scarlet military banners is immensely tranquil.

RIGHT Visitors are warned that the ascent to the castle is strenuous. The Pilgrims' Steps are the original route to the Mount.

BELOW And here is a good place to pause, with the sea showing darker shades of turquoise for different depths. The two gun batteries cover a cleft in the cliffs and once fired successfully on Cromwell's troops during the Civil War. The cleft is known as Cromwell's Passage.

LEFT And up again to the West entrance, set in the thickest walling of the castle. The St Aubyn's arms are above the Tudor doorway. During the sixteenth and seventeenth centuries this part of the castle used to be the Captain's quarters.

RIGHT The old Garrison or Guard Room lies below Chevy Chase, and has also adapted itself to different times. From Victorian days until 1976 it was used as a living room for footmen and junior servants.

The Church, founded on the highest rock of the Mount, is used regularly for public worship. The present building is mainly fourteenth century and probably stands on the masonry of Abbot Bernard's twelth-century priory. A religious community is mentioned in the Domesday Book of 1086, and there was one here in Saxon times.

RIGHT Under the family pews on the right side of the chancel, down a stone stairway, is a little dungeon. A man's skeleton was found there in the nineteenth century. In life he would have been over seven feet tall. Perhaps the legends of giants are created from the unusual height of such men as these.

LEFT A gilt candelabrum portraying the Virgin Mary and Child and St Michael slaying the dragon.

Sir John St Aubyn, 3rd baronet, a man of great taste and culture, brought eighteenth-century elegance to this part of the castle. During the 1760s the Lady Chapel, which had fallen into a state of decay, was transformed into the Blue Drawing Rooms. And though they now have a sociable instead of monastic purpose it seems apt that their atmosphere is feminine and their chosen colour the blue of the Virgin Mary's mantle.

LEFT This majestic pair of Italian vases in jasper and alabaster have been in the room since it was finished and furnished more that two centuries ago, and their alto-reliefs — in the words of Dr Borlase, tutor to the 4th baronet in the eighteenth century — depict *Hymeneal happiness fit to adorn the largest and most magnificent saloon.*

LEFT The door of the outer Blue Drawing Room stands
tantalisingly open, so that we can glimpse the inner one,
which may be seen but not entered, due to lack of space.
Yellow blinds are drawn down against the sun.
Architecturally, you are looking at a classic example of
Strawberry Hill Gothic — a style made famous by Sir Horace
Walpole, who built his ideal home at Strawberry Hill.

BELOW Herbert Hughes took this photograph in 1911,
showing St Michael's Mount as seen from Marazion quay,
with the causeway covered.

MORE BOSSINEY BOOKS ...

AROUND & ABOUT THE SMUGGLERS' WAYS
by David Mudd
Working through almost forty different sources, including the records of H.M. Customs & Excise itself, David Mudd (who discovered in the course of his research that his great-grandfather was a Customs officer) has produced a book that is as heady and addictive as the spirits, the wines and the tobaccos that once followed fish, tin and copper as Cornwall's great industries. Several of the sketches and many of the photographs are by David's wife, Diana.
'... scrapes the romantic glitter from Cornwall's erstwhile illicit trade ... Meticulously researched and written in David Mudd's lively factual style it makes absorbing reading.'
Alison Poole, Leader Group of Newspapers

MOUNT'S BAY
by Douglas Williams
In words and pictures Douglas Williams takes us from Land's End to Lizard Light, the most westerly and southerly point of Cornwall, enclosing a bay 'as majestic as any in Europe.'

DAPHNE DU MAURIER COUNTRY
by Martyn Shallcross
A special look at Cornwall in which the internationally-famous novelist set important stories.
'A treasure chest for those who love Cornwall and the du Maurier novels.'
Valerie Mitchell, The Packet Group of Newspapers

MY CORNWALL
A personal vision of this Celtic land by eleven writers: Daphne du Maurier, Ronald Duncan, James Turner, Angela du Maurier, Jack Clemo, Denys Val Baker, Colin Wilson, C.C. Vyvyan, Arthur Caddick, Michael Williams and Derek Tangye with reproductions of paintings by Margo Maeckelberghe and splendid black and white photographs.
'An ambitious collection of chapters.'
The Times, London

THE CRUEL CORNISH SEA
by David Mudd, 65 photographs
David Mudd selects more than 30 Cornish shipwrecks, spanning 400 years, in his fascinating account of seas and a coastline that each year claim their toll of human lives.
'This is an important book.'
Lord St Levan, The Cornish Times

CASTLES OF CORNWALL
by Mary and Hal Price, 78 photographs and map.
St Catherine's Castle and Castle Dore both at Fowey, Restormel near Lostwithiel, St Mawes, Pendennis at Falmouth, St Michael's Mount, Tintagel, Launceston amd Trematon near Saltash. Mary and Hal Price on this tour of Cornwall explore these nine castles.
'... a lavishly illustrated narrative that is both historically sound and written in a compelling and vivid style that carries the reader along from one drama to the next.'
Pamela Leeds, The Western Evening Herald

We shall be pleased to send you our catalogue giving full details of our growing list of titles for Devon, Cornwall, Dorset, Somerset and Wiltshire as well as forthcoming publications. If you have any difficulty in obtaining our titles, write direct to Bossiney Books, Land's End, St Teath, Bodmin, Cornwall.